The Absolute Spin...

Music Defines the Moment!

Why Selecting the Right Entertainment for Your Event Protects Your Investment

Ken Rochon, Jr.

The Absolute Spin...
Music Defines the Moment!

© 2015 by Ken Rochon, Jr.

1st Edition

ISBN: 978-1-942688-10-5

Printed in the United States of America

Contents

UNIT 4 – Doctorate in Fun

Appendix

Acknowledgements & Dedication

To my prodigy son DJ K3.

To my wife who has supported the Absolute Dream even when others quit.

To Gordon Thorn for the longest friendship and partnership I could ask for. You are my real brother.

To John Paul Berry Jr. for being a great friend and partner for three decades.

To Gary Rasmussen for being the brother and partner needed to keep this legacy alive. Twelve is a lucky number, and you joined as a partner and President of the company at your twelfth year performing as a deejay at Absolute.

To all the people over the years who have worked and kept Absolute Entertainment the longest running entertainment company in the Baltimore – Washington Metropolitan area. To all the deejays and staff members from back in the day to the current roster who have helped entertain over 25,000 events that caused many a wedding to be one of the best days of our clients lives. This list could easily be over 150 deejays, but I would like to focus on the ones who stood out as leaders. I'm proud that a lot of these leaders went on to start their own deejay companies and I hope what they learned at Absolute served them well; not just as a professional deejay, but as a way of living with integrity.

Here is a small sample of the greatness that shaped Absolute Entertainment over its 32 year reign: Adam Dutch Durham, Aditya 'Gotu Desai, Bill Marsh, Brandon Renninger, Brian Douglas, Brian Starkloff, Cedric Teamer, David Richardson, Devin Bradley, Ean McNaney, Evan Reitmeyer, Gavin O'Leary, Insa Ndiaye, Jacob Jenson, James Taavon, Jami Hampton Grant, Jason Canaan, Jason Wallace, Jeff Barbi, Jennifer Reitmeyer, Joe Munson, John Bird Armetta, Josh Levine, Keith Phillips, Kevin Flowers, Kim Brannan, Kyle Barker, Michael Greenberg, Morgan Williams, Nola Jae, Olu Akinsanya, Paul Hairston, Paul Love, Peter Kuyatt, Randy Richmond, Rio Hiett, Roderick Horried, Ryan Walburn, Steve Hartka, Tim Brown & too many more to list.

Special thanks to the leaders in the wedding industry who supported AE: Dan Wecker, Drew Vanlandingham, Eric Stocklin, Jay Buck, Jerry Edwards, John Zito, Karen Buck, Marc McIntosh, Max Major, Michael Tabrizi, Tula Stamas.

And to the 50,000 brides and grooms allowing us to be a part of their big day and trusting us to create it with love.

Lastly, to my publishing partner Al Granger and our team Carolyn Sheltraw and Sarah Coolidge.

Preface

Dear Bride, Groom, MOB (Mother of the Bride), FOB (Father of the Bride), caterer, event planner, fellow wedding industry professional, and concerned citizen for event success,

First of all congratulations on finding your partner for life. It is the most beautiful feeling to be in love and to celebrate it with your family and friends! The key is to make sure you will be celebrating your love and not regretting hiring the wrong deejay/entertainment choice that chases your guests away with bad decisions, bad equipment, bad judgment and bad talent. All this is avoidable, and this book shows you how.

I have always wanted to write this book and finally am downloading my brain to help save loved ones from experiencing an under whelming experience at their event. Since it is so avoidable, it should be easy to explain.

This book will show you some simple ways to make better choices with your entertainment, which will ultimately impact the celebration, fun, investment, and ultimately the success of your event.

The formula for this decision is logical, but most people don't know this formula exists or how to make sure the values they plug in are accurate. This book gives you that guidance and so many more secrets to making sure you and your guests have fun. And the bonus is that we have developed many music lists that have been regarded among the best of the best, so we know exactly how to apply this formula.

Happy reading!

Ken

Carpe Music
The Story

Little did I know that moving to Maryland my senior year of high school in 1982 would inspire me to become a deejay and start my first company. Thirty-two years later, AbsoluteEntertainment (AE) is still rockin' and has been the entertainment for over 20,000 weddings (that is a lot!!). Many of the top caterers, photographers, planners, and other vendors in the wedding industry have considered AE an innovator and leader in this industry.

In thirty-two years, I personally have performed and emceed over 2,000 weddings (which is over 60 weddings a year on average). I remember some years I deejayed as many as 125 weddings which was accomplished by doing 'doubles' on a Saturday, one wedding on a Friday night and one on a Sunday. Talk about being in shape!

I couldn't find another career or job that gave me more meaning and satisfaction. I was responsible for taking the entire budget, efforts, energy, and vision of my bride and groom and creating the best mood, so that the event would go by without anyone looking at their watch; everyone would just enjoy themselves. I was trusted to take all of the money and time they invested into this event and turn it into the best day of their lives.

It requires a lot of commitment and focus to do this consistently. It also takes a lot of creativity. No bride and groom are the same, so making the effort to make each event unique not only sets it apart, but results in a deep connection with the bride and groom and their guests. Quite frankly, if I didn't spend hours of preparation, I would probably have quit deejaying after three or four years because of boredom. My competitive side drives me to make an even greater mood impact at each event. And understanding how each mood builds on the previous mood almost guarantees a full dance floor.

I fell in love with deejaying because I was a music collector and needed to justify my addiction to investing in my albums (and later cd's and now iTunes). My Father was pretty sure I would outgrow this hobby, but I insisted that this was the only thing I knew I wanted to do. When you love what you do, it isn't a job and that is why ranking on the top of all the referral lists came naturally. We were on the preferred entertainment lists of the top hotels, mansions, Naval Academy, etc. which allowed us to focus on our craft. We were always committed to customers and knew if we consistently delivered a full dance floor and great music to set the mood, that we would get

5 star reviews on our surveys as well as on "The Knot" and "Wedding Wire". Today we have more 5 star reviews than any other deejay service. This is not by accident or luck. It is the art, the science and the strategy of understanding how to listen and deliver what our clients want.

Wedding planners who have been hired by a bride and groom from different cultures turn to us to mix the beats of different genres, creating a global melting pot on the dance floor.

What is the importance of having an incredible DJ? Music defines the moment. Having an amazing DJ can make your wedding/event an absolute success. On the other hand, having an ill-equipped, inexperienced DJ can make your wedding/event a nightmare. Your DJ has the ability to get the crowd dancing, lift the mood, and make your night one that your guests will be talking about long after it is over. With so many DJ options out there, you may be feeling overwhelmed or not know where to start when choosing the perfect fit. We have written this guide to ease your worries and give you absolute peace of mind when choosing your DJ.

Music defines the moment.

— Ken Rochon

Unit 1
Research

The true orchestration of mood

is the ultimate escape of time

— Ken Rochon

Bridal Shows, Social Media & Websites

Today it is easy to use the internet to learn more about who would be the best person to emcee your wedding and orchestrate the flow and mood of your big day.

My recommendation is to look at reviews much like you would if you were on Amazon deciding among several hundred companies. Who has the most five star experiences? What are people who were not happy with their experience saying about them? What is the proportion of success?

My top site recommendation would be WeddingWire, followed by a fan page on Facebook. After that, I would see if they are on recommendation lists for the locations you are considering for holding your reception. Finally, I would attend bridal shows to see how they handle themselves offline.

The number one way to make your final selection is to visit their office and experience a demo. Without a demo, everything you want will be agreeable and theoretical. The beauty of the demo is you get to experience and feel what talent the deejay has in creating mood. More about this in the chapter 'Coffee Cup vs. DJ Demo'

Customer Service

When it comes down to the single most important way to hire your deejay/entertainment/talent, it should be how committed they are to customer service. As stated earlier, their ratings on WeddingWire are a great indication of their ability to satisfy your needs and help you realize your vision of your big day.

If you are not being listened to, chances are your event will not be customized to your liking. This is a big indicator that the deejay is either not capable of altering his approach or style or that he doesn't care what you have to say.

What has made our company most successful is listening and taking notes about your expectations and specific artists that will help color the approach and mood to your event. Since every bride and groom is unique, it would really be impossible for a deejay to assume you are like all other brides and grooms and should just deal with the strategy he has for getting your dance floor full.

Take-aways from this short chapter are; make sure you are being listened to, make sure your expectations and songs are being noted and, most important, please make sure they can create the desired mood with your customized list or vision of your event.

Reviews & Results

Imagine a caterer saying to you 'Our food is the best!' and you respond 'Great, can I try it?' only to have them try to assure you that it is not necessary to experience the delicious food until your wedding day. Hiring a caterer without trying the food, hiring a photographer without seeing his photography, or hiring any other person without seeing their work would be crazy!

This may seem straight forward, but there are some tricks to expose the true skills and talents of the deejay you are considering so you don't fall into the trap of perception not equaling reality.

First of all, make sure you use WeddingWire because it contains feedback from real brides and grooms. Second, make sure it is not luck that the deejay or company has a high rating. In other words, make sure they have done a lot of events and been around a long time so that consistency and social proof equals reality.

Don't judge a deejay by his looks, charm or ability to have an answer for every question you have. It is very easy to say 'yes, I do that'. It is quite another thing to show that you do what you say.

For instance, it is easy to say you have all the music in the world, the best sound system and that you are a great mixer, etc. Ask the deejay to allow you to experience this. Without the result you desire being created, you are taking a huge chance of being disappointed on your wedding day.

Unit 2
Decisions

The best investment of money and time in a wedding is to achieve the outcome that time is forgotten, family and friends are drenched and exhausted from dancing, and your love has been celebrated beyond your wildest dreams.

— Ken Rochon

Band vs. DJ

Advantages and Disadvantages of using a Band	Advantages and Disadvantages of using a DJ
Bands are more expensive	DJs are less expensive
Higher chance that something could go wrong	If something goes wrong with DJ, they can readjust
Tend to be more unreliable	A DJ can play a huge variety of music

Music can change the world
because it can change people.

— Bono

Coffee vs. Music ...
That is the Question

It might be silly to demonstrate such an obvious difference... but this is what is happening in the deejay wedding industry. Scary!

Can you imagine if you called up a photographer and asked him to meet you about your wedding photography and he suggested that you meet with him at the local coffee café. You agree and when you arrive to see the photos he presents you with a cup of coffee. You accept and then ask if you may see his photos and he says "Wouldn't you rather drink this coffee? Isn't this coffee excellent? If you love this coffee, then you will love my photography work". Okay, that meeting would have been a total waste of your time, and so would meeting your caterer for a cup of coffee instead of experiencing a tasting.

You know that the music is important for the success of your event but how do you evaluate your deejay to know you and your guests will enjoy themselves?

Simple (hint: it has nothing to do with a cup of coffee)... we call this experience a must for selecting your professional disc jockey. It is a **"customized music demonstration"**.

Benefits:

You are able to communicate your music preferences and **experience** the music you select and how it will be incorporated into your ceremony, cocktail, dinner, and dancing.

You experience the sound system for clarity and fidelity as well as the **volume level.** We offer systems with dual volume levels so that your dancing guests will experience a full body sound while your guests conversing at the tables experience a social volume.

There is no practicing or experimenting with regard to your preferences on your wedding day, because the demo serves as a testing location for what works and doesn't work for you.

There is a lot to be said for privacy. Have you ever noticed how loud coffee shops are? At your customized music demonstration you are able to communicate without distractions what you and your guests will want to experience on your big day.

Café vs. Office… When a deejay wants to meet with you in a coffee shop it is because there is no office…and when a deejay is doing this part time, do you think they are invested in your big day? We are **full-time,** 7 days a week focusing on weddings and events. It is our only business, and we are **passionate** about it. This will be evident when you visit our office.

You are able to **feel confident** about your professional disc jockey company because you've just experienced your wedding instead of a cup of Joe.

"MUSIC Defines THE Moment!"

One good thing about music,

when it hits you, you feel no pain.

— Bob Marley

Solo DJ vs.
DJ Company

A big issue with DJ Solo is what happens if DJ Solo gets in an accident, is sick, or heaven forbid goes out of business. If DJ Solo is affected, there is a 100% chance his clients will also be affected. DJ Solo will typically state 'I never get sick' or 'I have a friend that will cover my event'.

The first response is plausible if DJ Solo has an amazing super human immune system, but the second is most likely a lie or very big stretch of the truth. I don't know any talented deejay who is sitting around waiting for his talented deejay friend to get sick so he can saddle up and save the day.

Thus, it is important to hire a company for many reasons. First and foremost, there is a backup plan. The company should have an emergency deejay assigned for every time slot so that when the inevitable happens, there is a real back up plan. Yours truly is one of the emergency deejays at our company because our staff shares the responsibility for making sure our weekends will be backed up with solutions for potential problems.

Secondly, a solid DJ company also has multiple sound systems, so they can have a rotation of sound systems being repaired and professional back up equipment.

My favorite reason for choosing a DJ company for your event is that there is a diversity of styles and talent. Not every deejay is right for every event. There is always one on the team that stands out as the best solution to the music preferences and style the bride and groom are asking for at their event.

Unit 3
Explanations & Expectations

Formulas for DJ (Hire)

(DJ) = Deejay (E) = Equipment (M) = Music (S) = Success

$$ (DJ) \times (E) \times (M) = (S) $$

So if the (DJ) is okay 7

The (E) is okay 7

The (M) is okay 7

(S) = 343

So if the (DJ) is okay 8

The (E) is okay 8

The (M) is okay 8

(S) = 512

However if your (DJ) is the best 10

But the (E) doesn't work 0

and the (M) was the best 10

(S) = 0

If your (DJ) is excellent 10

(E) is 10

(M) is 10

(S) = 1000

Thus if any of the 3 variables are zero the event is a failure.

For a wedding I would strongly advise you make sure that your
S is no lower than 512
(average of 8)

Some other variables to consider to determine the level of your deejay

CS X **EXP** X **KNOW** X **MIX** X **PRO** X **READ** = **DJ**

CS = Customer Service Oriented

MIX = Mixing Ability

PRO = Professionalism

EXP = Experience

READ = Ability to Read a Crowd

KNOW = Music Knowledge

Again if any of these variables are low or a zero, your event will be negatively impacted and possibly a failure.

Music is the soundtrack of your life.

— Dick Clark

DJ – The Coordinator

When you have a coordinator or event planner, then the deejay is the support and voice of that person in charge. But when there is no one in charge, you need your deejay to have that ability to be a leader.

You will not enjoy yourself if you have to be the coordinator at your own event. The experienced deejay doesn't need very much guidance to make good decisions. He/she will know that the flow of the event is crucial for your maximum enjoyment. Without this skill set in place, your deejay will cause the event to be boring and/or stressful. In other words, he/she can destroy your event because they don't know how to take charge and make things happen so that you and your guests enjoy themselves.

The best deejay is a team player and makes things happen behind the scenes so that what is experienced is enjoyable and natural.

Where words fail, music speaks.

— Hans Christian Andersen

DJ – The Mixologist

Not an alcohol mixer, but a music mixer! You will most likely have a bartender taking care of the drinks. A mixologist is blending music seamlessly so that a groove and mood are being created.

The only way to know if a deejay is a mixologist is to experience a demo or see them at an event.

Beware of the deejay that invites you to another bride's event! He will be focused on you instead of the bride. This means at your wedding, that there may be a prospective client he invites to your event that steals the attention and time you have paid for.

The policy of a professional deejay service is that a demo will be created for you to experience how talented they are at mixing music and creating mood first-hand.

*Music happens to be an art form
that transcends language.*

— Herbie Hancock

DJ – The Voice (Emcee)

Just like coordinating is leadership and mixing is artistry of beats and mood, being an emcee is a skill set quite unique from the others. Being a professional emcee means that you are confident, yet have enough humility to not grand stand at an event where the focus should be on the bride and groom. And the focus should be appropriate, sincere and timely.

The clarity of the emcee is essential for your guests to know what is going on. Make sure your deejay has a professional microphone, because it is also a big factor on the clarity of the announcements.

Some emcees forget they are at a wedding and sound more like they are hyping up the crowd for a worldwide wrestling match or that they are a radio jockey with their pompous insincere commentary.

Most brides want class and elegance which speaks to the emcee meaning what they say and not saying any more than they mean or need to. Sincerity is a quality of true connection. A deejay that is sincere will connect with a crowd and the crowd will connect more with this quality than any other.

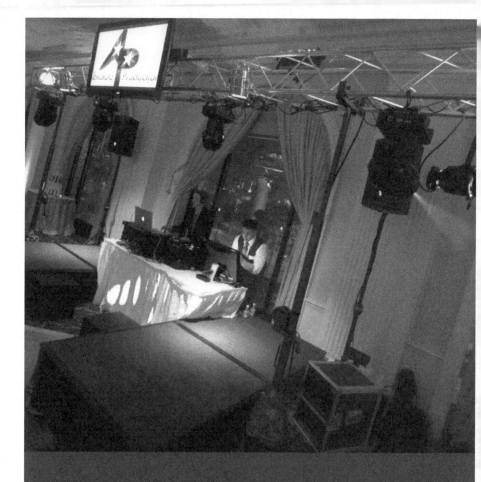

Unit 4
Doctorate in Fun

Music doesn't lie. If there is something to be changed in this world, then it can only happen through music.

-Jimi Hendrix

Flow & Sequence

Generally speaking a wedding is divided into four parts.

The Ceremony – One hour total. Thirty minutes for guest arrival and 30 minutes for actual ceremony

The Cocktail Hour – One hour (imagine that!)

The Dinner – One hour typically starts with welcome, blessing and toast(s), (some brides and grooms want to do some dancing during this portion because dinner service has typically three breaks (salad, entree, coffee)).

Dancing – Two hours or more. There is typically a break between hour one and hour two of the dancing to cut the cake, dance with parents, anniversary song, bouquet and garter toss, etc.

Each hour should have an announcement to keep guests aware of what is happening and the music should change to compliment the mood of that hour.

Dinner is the only hour that includes two distinct moods. The first mood is very elegant and compliments the dining experience, and the latter half of the dinner hour should start to mimic the cocktail hour in that it adds energy (foot tapping) to anticipate the dancing hour fast approaching.

Human Behavior & Psychology of Energy & Fun

It is most interesting to me the correlation of mood and behavior and how the art and science of music can create a shift in human behavior that is contagious.

The biggest difference between a talented deejay and a novice deejay is how they create the mood that compliments the time of the event. For instance, if a novice deejay plays dinner music during cocktail time, the mood is very serene and boring. It psychologically plays into the subconscious that the event will be boring and slow and thus people will sit in their seats longer and think about what time the event is over and when it would be appropriate to leave.

When the right mood is set each hour, the subconscious mind escapes and is preparing to have fun much sooner. There is more connection, more laughter, more anticipation of everyone letting loose and having fun on the dance floor. In other words, the careful selections of music during the ceremony, cocktail and dinner more quickly prepares guests to dance and party.

A professional deejay that sets this feeling up will have people during dinner come up and ask when the dancing is going to happen. Their subconscious is becoming very aware that they are having a lot of fun and want to express it physically. And that is why events with a professional deejay will create a sense of urgency to party at the end of dinner. There is literally a shift and movement of people rushing to the dance floor.

Music Defines
the Moment
Mixology & Mood

Not to beat a dead horse, but if you don't have the right mood at a given hour, then you have your guests looking at their watches or playing on their phones because they are bored. If a deejay has a certain set list they use at all events, I can assure you this will not work to create excitement.

A blend of standards with innovation and unpredictable cool music is the key to keeping most guests happy. They feel connected by music everyone knows AND they are pleasantly surprised by unpredictable cool songs they may or may not have ever heard before.

I approach all my events as if there is a blank canvas and I have either been guided with some of the paint colors that will be utilized or I have been trusted to read the crowd and pick the best paint (music) to create the best painting (full dance floor).

Music is my religion.

~Jimi Hendrix

Appendix

Music in the soul can be

heard by the universe.

~ Lao Tzu

DJ Agreement

AbsoluteEntertainment.com

professional entertainment and production services

7513 Connelley Drive I Suite K I Hanover I Maryland I 21076

Phone: 410.761.1212
Toll-Free: 800.252.5274
Fax: 410.761.5212
email: contactus@absoluteentertainment.com

Contract Number: 68044
Date of Offer: 1/11/2016
Expiration Date:

Agreement to Perform

AbsoluteEntertainment.com hereby agrees to provide professional entertainment services for the following:

Sponsor's Name:

Event Name:

Event Description:

Event Date:

Event Time: -

Event Location:

Event Address:

Event Location Phone Number:

Price:

Deposit (minimum 50%): _____ due upon signing

Balance : _____ due by 1/11/2016

Terms and Conditions

Reservations and Programming

AbsoluteEntertainment.com will reserve verbally requested dates for up to three weeks pending the return of this agreement signed and accompanied by the deposit specified **at least four weeks prior to the event date**. To ensure appropriate programming, the sponsor must also return the event/wedding questionnaire, directions, and MusicMix request form by 1/11/2016.
AbsoluteEntertainment.com will not be held responsible for reservations, as sealed by the return of agreement, or programming requests received less than four weeks in advance of the event date. Specifically requested personnel must be written in at time of contract offer otherwise personnel will be assigned based on paperwork provided to us by client four (4) weeks prior to event date.

_____   _____   _____   _____
AbsoluteEntertainment.com   Date   Authorizing Signature of: Date

Organization:

Fax:

Absolute Excitement   **Absolute Fun**   **Absolute Value**

The Absolute Spin **43**

Environmental and Sponsor Support Requirements

AbsoluteEntertainment.com disc jockeys will work hard to ensure your event's success. To help them along, we ask that you, the sponsor, provide a minimum level of shelter and sustenance to protect our sound systems and keep our humans happy in their work.

Shelter --- The sponsoring person or organization of an event taking place out-of-doors will provide **overhead shelter** sufficient to repel both sun and rain.

Sustenance --- The sponsoring person or organization will provide **nonalcoholic beverages and a meal** (when appropriate) to AbsoluteEntertainment.com personnel either before or within the first hour of the event program.

Tables --- The sponsoring person or organization will provide **two banquet or 6-foot tables** to support Absolute Sounds' equipment. If such support cannot be provided, AbsoluteEntertainment.com will attach a $50 drayage charge to the total bill with payment due within 30 days of the event.

Payment Due Dates and Cancellations

The sponsoring person or organization agrees to pay the deposit noted upon signing this contract and to provide the balance due 30 days in advance of the date of the event. Failure to complete payment on the date specified will result in collection remedies, not disincluding legal action by counsel, the costs of which will be reimbursed by the sponsor. In addition, AbsoluteEntertainment.com will charge interest on past due bills at the rate of 2 percent per month.

Cancellations brought about by inclement weather will obtain the refund of the deposit minus an administrative and reservation fee of $150 (the reservation of an alternate event date following cancellation due to inclement weather will be based on availability as determined by AbsoluteEntertainment.com and the new date must be booked within 30 days of the cancelled event). Cancellations received **in writing** more than 30 days from the performance date will only be responsible for the deposit being paid and cleared of any obligation for balance. Cancellations not received in writing or received 30 days or less prior to the event date will require full payment of the performance agreement. Additional equipment (to include lights, speakers, etc) are nonrefundable thirty (30) days after signed contract date.

Damage to AbsoluteEntertainment.com Equipment or Persons

The sponsoring person or organization here undersigned will be held responsible for any damages to AbsoluteEntertainment.com equipment or personnel resulting from the misconduct of any associated agents or guests, and compensation for such damages will be paid to AbsoluteEntertainment.com within the ten days following the event date. Failure to provide such compensation within the period so noted will result in collection remedies, including recourse to counsel, the costs of which will be reimbursed by the sponsor.

By the signatures affixed below, AbsoluteEntertainment.com and the sponsoring person or organization hereby mutually agree to the terms of this contract. Additional commitments will not be binding unless they are written and signed by both contracting parties. The validity of this contract is sealed by the authorizing signatures of both parties contained herein.

| AbsoluteEntertainment.com | Date | Authorizing Signature of: | Date |

Organization:

Address:

Work Phone:

Home Phone:

Fax:

Please indicate method of payment and amount below:

☐ Check
☐ Visa
☐ MasterCard
☐ Discover
☐ American Express

CARD NUMBER

$ ☐☐☐☐.☐☐
AMOUNT OF YOUR CHECK OR CHARGE

SECURITY CODE

EXPIRATION DATE

Absolute Excitement   Absolute Fun   Absolute Value

DJ Decisions
Dancing, Drinking, Eating & Tipping

This is the most controversial section of the book and my opinions are derived from 32 years of experience studying what works and what doesn't.

I believe if you allow your deejay to dance, you are losing your deejay. Most deejays would never do this, but if one does join the guests on the floor it begs the question: who is running the event? Some 'deejays' are not professional. A professional deejay is at your event to work to create the event you hired him or her to create. Deejays that are there to hook up, pick up and basically be paid to party with your guests are not only unprofessional but, they will ultimately affect your wedding because there isn't a focus on your event.

Drinking for the most part is a no-no. That isn't to say that a deejay who drinks will ruin your event, it is just a point again of professionalism and potentially compromising the event because of a lack of clarity and focus. Making announcements, coordinating, and mixing music takes a lot of concentration. I am sure one or two drinks will not affect the outcome of the event, in fact it may actually loosen the deejay up to create a better event. The question is: 'Have you hired an experienced, seasoned pro that doesn't need to be told this or have you hired a person who is negligent and unprofessional and will expect to drink freely?'

Eating is a yes-yes. :) Most brides and grooms want their entertainment and photographers and site team to eat. After all, a deejay will be working from eight to ten hours from the time he leaves his home or office to the time he finishes. The problem lies in when you feed your deejay. Unfortunately, this is one of the biggest oversights in the industry. The best caterers know to feed the talent at the same time as the guests so they are done and ready to go when it is time for first dance or whatever is next. The oblivious caterers do not care if the talent eats because they are only focused on the bride and groom and guests. They forget that the talent is a necessary part of the team and is an extension of the bride and groom.. It is vital you have your talent fed at the same time as the guests and preferably at the beginning of the dinner hour so that can actually get back to work as soon as possible. A common wedding malfunction for deejays is to wait to be fed only to be told to gorge themselves because they only have two minutes until the first dance.

Most brides do not know they are paying for the talent to eat and that their event would be enhanced if the talent were fed early. Lastly, vendor meals are typically a waste of money as some of your guests will not show up and those meals can easily be repurposed for the talent. If you buy a vendor meal and four guests don't show up, typically the vendor meals are served and the regular meals are eaten by the catering staff or wasted.

To tip or not to tip... This is the easiest decision. Did your deejay exceed your expectations? Did they keep everyone at your event, dancing and happy, and did you forget about time? Did your guests rave about the music and the great time they had? If the answer is 'Yes' to any or all of these questions, then a tip is appropriate. Mind you, it is not required and in most cases not expected. But tips with thank you cards are a classy way to express your gratitude and are deeply appreciated.

Next to the Word of God,

the noble art of music is the

greatest treasure in the world.

— Martin Luther

Music & Specialty Dances

Ceremony

Air on the G String
All You Need is Love – Vitamin String Quartet
Ave Maria
Bittersweet Symphony – Vitamin String Quartet
Chasing Cars – Vitamin String Quartet
Four Seasons
Hallelujah – Vitamin String Quartet
I'm Yours – Vitamin String Quartet
In My Place – Vitamin String Quartet
Jesu, The Joy of Man's Desiring
Never Tear Us Apart – Vitamin String Quartet
Pachelbel's Canon in D
The Prince of Denmark
Sunrise, Sunset
Trumpet Voluntary
The Wedding March from Midsummer Night's Dream
The Wedding Song
You're My Best Friend – Vitamin String Quartet
Your Love is King – Vitamin String Quartet
Your Song – Vitamin String Quartet

Cocktail

Aloe Blacc – The Man
The Band – The Weight
Belle & Sebastian – If She Wants Me
Billy Joel – Piano Man
Zac Brown Band – Chicken Fried
Bruno Mars – Marry You
The Chainsmokers & Coldplay – Something Just Like You
Common Kings – Take Her
Dave Brubeck Quartet – Take Five
Dean Martin – Sway (Quien Sera)
DJ Jazzy Jeff & The Fresh Prince – Summertime
Kaleo – Way Down We Go
Kygo – Here for You
Kygo & Selena Gomez – It Aint Me
Lola Marsh – Wishing Girl
Marian Hill – Down
Matisyahu – One Day
Nat King Cole – L-O-V-E
Novika – Miss Mood (Satin Jackets Remix)
Passenger – Let Her Go (Kygo Remix)
Mr. Probz – Waves (Robin Schulz Radio Edit)
Van Morrison – Moondance
Ed Sheeran – Shape of You
Thievery Corporation – Lebanese Blonde
What So Not – High You Are (Branchez Remix)

Other Suggestions:
Michael Buble, Bob Marley, Dave Matthews Band, Doors,
    Frank Sinatra, Steely Dan, UB40

Best Jazz Artists

1. Louis Armstrong
2. Duke Ellington
3. Miles Davis
4. Charlie Parker
5. John Coltrane
6. Dizzy Gillespie
7. Billie Holiday
8. Thelonious Monk
9. Charles Mingus
10. Count Basie
11. Lester Young
12. Ella Fitzgerald
13. Coleman Hawkins
14. Sidney Bechet
15. Art Blakey
16. Bill Evans
17. Benny Goodman
18. Stan Getz
19. Sarah Vaughan
20. Herbie Hancock
21. Django Reinhardt
22. Dave Brubeck
23. Oscar Peterson
24. Wes Montgomery
25. J. J. Johnson
26. Artie Shaw
27. Chick Corea
28. Dexter Gordon
29. Chet Baker
30. Gerry Mulligan
31. Wynton Marsalis
32. Charlie Haden
33. Pat Metheny
34. Glenn Miller

RESOURCE
http://www.digitaldreamdoor.com

Dinner

Adele – Make You Feel My Love
Adele – Hello
Alphaville – Forever Young
Louis Armstrong – A Kiss to Build a Dream On
Beach Boys – God Only Knows
Beatles – Here, There and Everywhere
Eva Cassidy – Fields of Gold
Kenny Chesney – Me and You
Lana Del Rey – Summertime Sadness
Nick Drake – Northern Sky
Ben Folds – The Luckiest
Al Green – Lets Stay Together
Jem – Its Amazing
Billy Joel – Shes Got A Way
Elton John – Tiny Dancer
B.B. King & Eric Clapton – Come Rain or Come Shine

Other Suggestions:
Coldplay, Cure, Bryan Ferry, Ella Fitzgerald, Peter Gabriel,
    Billie Holiday

Introductions

2 Unlimited – Get Ready For This
AC/DC – Thunderstruck
Black Eyed Peas – Lets Get This Party Started
Chris Brown – Forever
Coldplay – A Sky Full of Stars
Phil Collins – In The Air Tonight
Rihanna ft. Calvin Harris – Now That We Found Love
U2 – Beautiful Day
Verve – Bitter Sweet Symphony'

1st Dances

Always & Forever – Heatwave
Broken Arrow – Rod Stewart
Calling You – Blue October
Can't Help Falling in Love – Elvis Presley
Faithfully – Journey
Fallen – Lauren Wood
Falling Slowly – Glen Hansard & Marketa Irglova
Forever Young – Rod Stewart
The Gift – Jim Brickman
Have I Told You Lately That I Love You – Van Morrison
How Deep is Your Love – Bee Gees
I Cross My Heart – George Strait
I Don't Want to Miss a Thing – Aerosmith
I Only Have Eyes For You – Flamingoes
I'm so in Love With You – Al Green
Je t'aime – Lara Fabian
Make You Feel My Love – Garth Brooks
A Man is in Love – Waterboys
My Valentine – Martina McBride & Jim Brickman
Nothing Has Ever Felt Like This – Rachelle Farrell & Will
    Downing
Never Felt This Way – Brian McKnight
Nothing Compares 2U – Sinéad O Connor
Por Amarte – Enrique Iglesias
Power of Love – Celine Dion
Right Here Waiting – Richard Marx
Share My Life – Kem
Sign Your Name – Terrence Trent D'Arby
So In Love – Cole Porter
Someone Like You – Van Morrison
Still the One – Shania Twain
Thinking Out Loud – Ed Sheeran
Unchained Melody – Righteous Brothers
You – Jesse Powell
Falling Slowly-Glen Hansard

Dances

Kyla La Grange – Cut Your Teeth (Kygo Remix)
Daddy Yankee – Limbo & Oye Mi Canto & Rompe & Que Tengo Que Hacer
Disclosure – Latch (feat. Sam Smith)
DJ Snake & Lil Jon – Turn Down for What
Earth Wind & Fire – September
Florida Georgia Line
David Guetta – Without You (feat. Usher)
Haddaway – What is Love
Calvin Harris – I Need Your Love (feat. Ellie Goulding) & Summer
Icona Pop – I Love It (feat. Charli XCX)
Jive Bunny – Swing the Mood
Journey – Dont Stop Believin
Michael Jackson – Billie JeanGlen Miller – In The Mood
Don Omar – Danza Kuduro (feat. Lucenzo) & Taboo & Zumba
Pharrell Williams – Happy
Pitbull – Dont Stop the Party & Give Me Everything & Timber & Hey Baby
Shakira – Hips Dont Lie & Umbrella
Tiesto – Red Lights
Usher – Yeah (feat. Lil Jon & Ludacris)
Wisin & Yandel – Algo Me Gusta De Ti & Me Estás Tentando

Other Suggestions:
Daft Punk, Flo Rida, Florida Georgia Line, Katy Perry, Maroon 5, Nicki Minaj, Robin Thicke

Line Dances

Brooks & Dunn – Boot Scootin' Boogie
Chicken Dance
Cupid – Cupid Shuffle
DJ Casper – Cha Cha Slide
Macarena
Marcia Griffiths – Electric Slide
Rednex – Cotton Eye Joe
Wobble

Old School

Apache – Sugar Hill Gang
Before I Let You Go – Frankie Beverly & Maze
I Know You Got Soul – Eric B. & Rakim
It Takes Two – Rob Base & DJ E-Z Rock
Joy and Pain – Rob Base & DJ E-Z Rock
Planet Rock – Afrika Bambaataa
Rapper's Delight – Sugar Hill Gang
In Da Club – 50 Cent
Country Grammar – Nelly
Lose Yourself – Eminem

Current

24K Magic – Bruno Mars
Classic (feat. Powers) – The Knocks
Cold Water (feat. Justin Bieber & Mo) – Major Lazer
Despacito (feat. Justin Bieber) [Remix] – Luis Fonsi &
    Daddy Yankee
Down – Marian Hill
Feels (feat. Pharrell Williams, Katy Perry & Big ... – Calvin
    Harris
HandClap – Fitz & The Tantrums
Heathens – twenty one pilots
Hello – Adele (Reggae Cover) – Conkarah & Rosie Delmah
Hymn for the Weekend (Seeb Remix) – Coldplay
I Feel It Coming (feat. Daft Punk) – The Weeknd
It Ain 't Me – Kygo & Selena Gomez
Lean on Like I can (remix mashup) – Sam Smith vs Major
    Lazer x DJ Snake
Let Me Love You (feat. Justin Bieber) – DJ Snake
Light It Up (feat. Nyla & Fuse ODG) [Remix] – Major
    Lazer
More Than You Know – Axwell A Ingrosso
MyWay – Calvin Harris
One Day – Matisyahu
Roses (feat. ROZES) – The Chainsmokers
Shape of You – Ed Sheeran
Shooting Stars – Bag Raiders
Something Just Like This – The Chainsmokers & Coldplay
Sorry – Justin Bieber
Stay – Zedd & Alessia Cara
Stressed Out – twenty one pilots
SUBEME LA RADIO (feat. Descemer Bueno, Zio ... –
    Enrique Iglesias

Take Her – Common Kings
There 's Nothing Holdin ' Me Back – Shawn Mendes
This Girl – Kungs & Gookin ' On 3 Burners
Turn Down For What – DJ Snake & Lil Jon
Unforgettable (feat. Swae Lee) B – French Montana
Way Down We Go – Kaleo
Wild Thoughts (feat. Rihanna & Bryson Tiller) D – DJ
  Khaled
Wishing Girl – Lola Marsh
Worth It (feat. Kid Ink) – Fifth Harmony

Specialty Dances

Father / Daughter

Al Martino – Daddy's Little Girl
Bob Carlisle – Butterfly Kisses
Celine DIon – Because You Loved Me
Fleetwood Mac – Landslide
Heartland – I Loved Her First
Loudon Wainwright III – Daughter
Paul Simon – Father and Daughter
Temptations – My Girl

Mother / Son

Boys II Men – Song for Mama
Kenny Rogers – Through the Years
Lee Ann Womack – I Hope You Dance
Louis Armstrong – What a Wonderful World
Rascal Flatts – My Wish

Cake Cutting

Archies – Sugar, Sugar
Average White Band – Cut the Cake
Beatles – When I'm 64
Cake – Love You Madly
Def Leppard – Pour Some Sugar On Me
James Taylor – How Sweet It Is (To Be Loved By You)
Queen – You're My Best Friend
Pat Benatar – Hit Me With Your Best Shot
Sarah Mclachlan – Ice Cream
U2 – Sweetest Thing

Sing-Along Songs

Africa – Toto
All That She Wants – Ace of Base
Call Me Maybe – Carly Rae Jepsen
Can't Get Enough of Your Love – Barry White
Cecilia – Simon & Garfunkel
Don't Stop Believin' – Journey
Footloose – Kenny Loggins
I Want It That Way – Backstreet Boys
Ice Ice Baby – Vanilla Ice
Jessie's Girl – Rick Springfield
Living on a Prayer – Bon Jovi
Love Shack – B52's
Mony Mony – Billy Idol
Sweet Caroline – Neil Diamond
You Shook Me All Night Long – AC/DC
You've Lost That Lovin' Feeling – Righteous Brothers
Your Love – Outfield

It is interesting to note that

a great deejay helps people

lose time as they celebrate love

~ Ken Rochon

Exclusivity Clause vs. Freedom to Capture Love

Freedom to Capture Love is a campaign born from a need to educate photographers and wedding clients of the dangers of an exclusivity clause as it pertains to social media. Obviously, there is a difference in being an event photographer and marketing a company on social media.

The following article was seen by over 65,000 people and became one of the top articles in Forbes that week for entrepreneurs.

Imagine planning your wedding and learning that an exclusivity clause in the photography contract prevented any of your family, friends and vendors from sharing the beauty of your day online. Worse, that a photographer can fine, sue or even walk off your wedding day because you breached your contract when you allowed someone else at your event to capture the love of your day.

This is an example of operating in a scarcity mentality and everyone involved is negatively affected. Our mission at

T.U.S. is to educate people on the beauty of collaboration and partnership. When we take pictures at a wedding (or any event for that matter) we establish with the client that we are there to promote the client, the event, the guests, the sponsors, the vendors and the photographers.

In the world of social media, it is about timing, and our experience is that professional photographers are great at their craft, but not aware of the power of marketing, social media and timing, which affects all the other vendors who created the event. It is a very bad decision to leave marketing to a non-marketer. Marketers are especially focused on making sure the world knows who the key players are in an event, a story or anything that is related to business branding, exposure and messaging.

The following article shares the story of what the dangers of an exclusivity clause are when you are planning an event that you want to share on social media. Regardless of the equipment, reason, or vendor, an exclusivity clause is taking away the 'Freedom to Capture Love'. So many people lose when we choose exclusivity and scarcity as a way to live life.

Questions to Ask Your Potential DJ

1. How many years of experience do you have? How long have you been in business?

2. How many weddings have you done?

3. Will you be the DJ at our wedding?

4. May we meet you in person before we sign a contract?

5. What makes your different from your competitors?

6. Have you played at our venue before?

7. What if something happens to you and you can't make it to the wedding?

8. Are you insured?

9. Why should I choose you as my wedding DJ?

10. Can I come see you at a wedding/event before I book your services? The answer should always be no. You wouldn't want some random couple crashing your wedding, would you?

11. What if we want to go past our end time?

You know what music is?
God's little reminder that
there's something else besides
us in this universe;
harmonic connection between
all living beings, everywhere,
even the stars.

— Robin Williams

About the Author

Ken Rochon founded Absolute Entertainment.com in 1982, and they have entertained over 25,000 events and weddings winning many industry awards for excellence. Ken is sought after for his mixing ability and understanding of world music. Ken has traveled to over 100 countries learning about culture and music. Performing over 2,500 weddings, he constantly looks for new ways to push the boundaries of using world music with current dance music. He has been a music collector for most of his life, and loves what music does for the soul.

Of music be the
food of love, play on.

— William Shakespeare

Leaders in the Industry

Music is the strongest form

of magic.

— Marilyn Manson

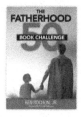

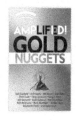

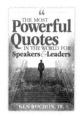

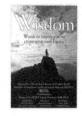

Made in USA - Kendallville, IN
1237200_9781942688105
02.22.2021 0918